Out of CONTROL

Alien Invaders

by **William Caper**

EPIDEMIC!

by **Lilly Golden**

GLOBE FEARON

Pearson Learning Group

Contents

Alien Invaders

Alien INVADERS

BY WILLIAM CAPER

CHAPTER 1
They're Here!

You have probably read science fiction books or seen movies that tell about Earth being invaded by creatures from other planets. These stories are fiction. Did you know, however, that parts of our planet are being invaded right now? The invaders are living organisms found right here on Earth.

An animal or a plant that settles into a new habitat is an invader. It lives in a place where it had not lived before. It is not a native. Such nonnative settlers are often described as foreign, transplanted, **exotic**, or even alien.

Depending on your point of view, or your **perspective**, a new species in a habitat can be a good or a bad thing. Say a beautiful new flower appears in a field. That can be nice if you want to decorate your dinner table with something unusual. Many new species that were not native to an area have been welcome additions. In the Americas, wheat, sugar cane, and coffee were all non-native plant species. In the animal kingdom, some species that were not native to these continents include horses, sheep, and cows. Europeans brought all of these species to the Americas about 300 years ago.

Sometimes, however, a new species might cause problems in its new habitat. It might compete for food with animals that live there. By gobbling up all the food available, the invaders put the native species at a great **disadvantage**. The habitat might not contain enough resources to **sustain** both. Another possible problem is that the invader might prey on native species. Invasive species can become an enormous problem for many local inhabitants, including people.

The scary truth is that invasions by alien species are on the rise. Invading organisms are one of the biggest threats to wildlife today. There are three basic kinds of invasion. One takes place by accident. For example, mussels attach themselves to the bottom of a boat. When the boat travels to a new destination, the **elusive**, or hard to reach, mussels may then drop off in the water—and into a new habitat.

Another kind of invasion is a planned one. Sometimes people deliberately carry a species beyond its native range and release it into a new environment. Farmers might do this because they want a new crop in their fields. Scientists might introduce a species that preys on an animal that has become a nuisance, in order to control its population. For example, the mongoose was introduced into Hawaii in 1883 to control rats.

The third kind of invasion also takes place when a new species is brought into a new area on purpose. In this case, though, the species is accidentally set loose in the environment. Say you buy an **exotic** snake as a pet. One day the snake escapes from your home. The snake survives, finds a mate, and reproduces. It has invaded a new habitat.

You will soon read about five invasive species causing serious problems—the snakehead fish, the kudzu vine, the brown tree snake, the coqui frog, and the zebra mussel. You'll learn the **circumstances** in which these invaders arrived in their new environment and you'll see how they affected it. You'll also see how people are trying to stop these aliens from taking over parts of Earth.

All these methods of travel can help invading species to spread. Can you guess how?

How can a fish
walk? Look for
clues in this photo.

CHAPTER **2**

Frankenfish

There is a freshwater pond in Crofton, Maryland, a small town not very far from Washington, D.C. In 2000, this pond had several different kinds of fish in it. Today, there is mostly one kind of fish in the pond—the northern snakehead fish. What happened to all of the other fish? The snakeheads have eaten them.

Snakeheads are not native to Maryland, or even to the United States. How did the snakeheads get to this pond in Maryland in the first place? The story you are about to read is a perfect example of a species being introduced because its owners set it free in the wild.

There are 28 different species of snakehead fish. They are all native to Asia and Africa. The northern snakehead is native to China. It can also be found in Korea and Russia. It usually grows to a length of about 33 inches. The northern snakehead's body is shaped like a cylinder and is generally brown or brown and tan.

Northern snakeheads like to live in shallow ponds and streams that have dense vegetation on the bottom. They have large mouths, sharp teeth, and big appetites. They mainly eat other fish. Sometimes they eat insects, shellfish, worms, tadpoles, adult frogs, and snakes. Some species of northern snakeheads have attacked and killed humans, especially people who went near the fish's babies. Yet, even though they defend their babies so fiercely, snakeheads sometimes eat them! That should give you an idea of how big an appetite this fish has.

The female northern snakehead can spawn, or reproduce, five times a year. She lays 1,000 to 15,000 eggs each time she spawns. Of course, not all of the babies survive.

When snakeheads run out of food, they will jump out of their pond and "walk" to another pond nearby. Of course, they don't really walk. They sort of hop on two strong fins. They can also breathe air, and they can survive out of water for several days if they stay moist. That's how the northern snakehead can travel over land from one body of water to another.

Some people find the idea of a fish leaping out of one pond and walking a little scary. That's why U.S. newspapers have nicknamed the northern snakehead "Frankenfish."

In Asia, snakeheads are a popular food item. They taste good and are excellent in soup. Live snakehead fish were shipped from Asia to the United States and sold by fish markets in Asian communities. Of all the species of live snakeheads sent to the United States, northern snakeheads were the most common. In 2002, people could easily buy live northern snakeheads in fish markets in New York and Boston. This invasion all started under very ordinary **circumstances**—with a desire to make soup. That's how the pond in Maryland wound up with snakeheads.

Terror in the Pond

A man from Hong Kong living in Crofton had a sister who was sick. The man decided to make her snakehead fish soup. In Hong Kong, many people believe snakehead fish soup can help heal a sick person.

The man called a fish market in New York and was sent two live northern snakeheads. However, before the fish arrived, his sister got well. So the man put the snakeheads in his home aquarium and fed them goldfish.

The snakeheads got bigger and bigger. Soon they were each eating six goldfish a day. Caring for the snakeheads was becoming an **economic** problem for the man, so he decided to take them to a pond and let them go.

In their new home, the snakeheads mated and had lots of babies. They also began to eat the other fish in the pond. Because northern snakeheads have no natural **predators** in North America, there was nothing to stop them or to control the pond's snakehead population. Snakeheads are what are known as top-level **predators**. That means they prey on other animals, but other animals do not prey on them.

Two years later, a man fishing in the pond caught what he thought was "a suspicious fish." He took a picture of the fish and sent it to wildlife authorities. An investigation was begun, and more snakeheads were found in the pond.

What should be done? There were other ponds nearby. Had any of the snakeheads climbed out of this pond and walked to the others? No one knew. There was also another problem. The Little Patuxent River was a short distance from the pond in Crofton. Had snakeheads reached that river? If they were in the Little Patuxent, they could reach other rivers. In this case, they wouldn't have to walk—they could swim!

A special panel was formed to study the problem. The panel considered using nets and traps to catch the snakeheads. It considered draining the ponds. It even thought about using explosives to kill the snakeheads. However, the panel decided there was no way to be sure that these methods would get rid of all the snakeheads. Finally, it concluded that the only sure way out of this **predicament** was to poison all the fish in this pond and the other ponds nearby.

After the poison had time to work, more than 120 dead snakeheads, mostly young ones, were removed from the pond. Other dead fish were also found. It was unfortunate that these other fish had to die. However, the snakeheads were considered to be such a **formidable** threat to native species that authorities were willing to sacrifice the other fish. They were even willing to risk destroying the **vitality** of the pond, so they could be sure they had eliminated all the snakeheads. Luckily, no snakeheads had reached other ponds or the Little Patuxent River.

Northern snakehead fish were found in this pond in Crofton, Maryland. What action did the authorities take after this terrifying discovery?

2125A

NO FISHING

A scientist who is an expert on snakeheads keeps two northern snakeheads in a tank by themselves in a laboratory in Florida. The snakeheads eat more than six fish every day. He says, "They're terrific **predators** with lots of teeth. This is not something you really want to see outside the laboratory."

Yet northern snakeheads are being seen outside the laboratory—in Florida and elsewhere. So is the bullseye snakehead, which is one of the largest snakehead species. This species can grow up to 6 feet long. Authorities think this fish may have been intentionally introduced as food. It also might have been bought by people for their home aquariums and then released.

Northern snakeheads have also been found in California and Massachusetts. Another species similar in size to the bullseye snakehead is the giant snakehead. This fish has been found in Maine, Massachusetts, Rhode Island, and Wisconsin. Like the snakehead found in Florida, these fish are thought to have been bought by people who first kept them as pets. When they became too big for their tanks or too expensive to feed, they were released into the wild.

Check out the sharp teeth on this baby northern snakehead.

In 2004, snakeheads were back in Maryland and in Virginia, too. This time they weren't in a pond. Northern snakeheads were found in the Potomac River, which flows through both of these states.

What's being done about the northern snakehead fish? Many states have made it illegal to own live snakeheads. In 2002, after the snakeheads were found in Maryland, the federal government **imposed** a ban on the trading and importing of all 28 species of snakeheads. It also declared it illegal to transport snakeheads from one state to another. However, some people **elude** the law and buy snakeheads illegally.

Snakeheads are a good example of how people help invasive species spread. According to the federal government, at least 185 species of **exotic** fish have been found in U.S. waters. More than half of them are fish from home aquariums.

Some people might think there's nothing wrong with releasing a few **exotic** fish into the wild. However, look at it from another **perspective**. What if those few northern snakeheads in Crofton had found their way into a large river instead of a small pond? What if they had established themselves as a large population? The U.S. Fish and Wildlife Service says that a large northern snakehead population would pose a major threat to many endangered species in the United States. It's estimated that a large northern snakehead population would endanger 16 species of amphibian, 5 species of crustacean, and 115 species of fish.

To control the spread of northern snakeheads, it's **vital** to find them before they establish large populations or move into additional bodies of water. However, the problem won't go away as long as people continue to buy and release snakeheads. As we will see with other invaders, humans are often the starring players in species invasion!

How can this
pretty vine be such
a menace?

CHAPTER 3
The Vine That Ate the South

Snakehead fish are famous for their large appetites. The next invasive species is also known for "eating," though it's not a fish or an animal—it's a vine. A vine is a kind of plant that climbs on things or extends along the ground. You may be wondering how a vine can eat. This plant, the kudzu vine, is known as "the vine that ate the South."

Of course, this vine didn't really eat the South. It just grew so fast there that it covered everything in its path. Kudzu has become so much a part of the South that many people don't realize that before 1876 this vine didn't exist anywhere in the United States. Like the snakehead fish, the kudzu vine is an introduced species. It was brought to the United States on purpose. Unlike the snakehead, it was brought here with the idea that it would become part of the environment. At the time, people didn't know the problems it would cause. Let's go back to the beginning of the kudzu's story.

A Versatile Plant

The kudzu vine is native to Asia. It has large green leaves and purple flowers when it blooms. In late summer, the sweet scent of kudzu blossoms floats on the air.

Kudzu grows with amazing **vitality**. It can grow up to a foot every day. No wonder it spreads so fast!

Kudzu was introduced into the United States in 1876. That year, a huge international fair called the Centennial Exposition was held in Philadelphia, Pennsylvania, to celebrate the nation's one-hundredth birthday. Many countries participated in the fair. The Japanese government built a garden with plants from Japan. One of those plants was kudzu. Kudzu served as an ornamental vine, and it provided shade for the Japanese exhibit.

Americans liked kudzu's large leaves and sweet-smelling blossoms. Some wanted this pretty, pleasant-smelling plant for their gardens. Many southern homeowners wanted to use kudzu to provide shade for their porches.

In Florida, a farmer discovered that his animals liked to eat kudzu. The word spread about kudzu's usefulness as forage. Plants that are grown as food for animals are called forage. The Florida farmer opened a plant nursery. During the 1920s, he sold kudzu plants by mail. People all around the country bought them.

During the 1930s, there was a serious drought in many parts of the United States. In some places, the soil had dried up, turned to dust, and been blown away. Could kudzu, with its thick roots that held soil in place, help in areas that were in danger of soil erosion? The U.S. government gave people jobs planting large fields of kudzu. Kudzu was still being used to control soil erosion in the 1940s.

A Miracle Vine?

During the 1940s, a man from Georgia named Channing Cope became convinced that kudzu was the key to stopping soil erosion in the South. Cope called kudzu "the miracle vine." He encouraged people to grow it. He wrote newspaper articles about kudzu, and he talked about it on radio programs. He traveled across the southeastern United States starting kudzu clubs. He helped to stage kudzu festivals and organize kudzu-planting contests. In the South, the most important crop had always been cotton. Cope liked kudzu so much that he told people, "Cotton isn't king here anymore. Kudzu is king!"

Cope wasn't the only person who thought kudzu was like a miracle for the South. For many of the poorer people in the South, kudzu was an answer to two **economic** problems. These problems were losing land to erosion and not having enough food for farm animals. By planting kudzu, people could **apparently** stop erosion and have food for their animals. Most people still didn't know what lay ahead.

Kudzu grows very well in the southern United States, perhaps even better than in its native habitat. One reason for its **vitality** is that the South's warm, wet climate is perfect for growing kudzu. Another reason is that kudzu's natural enemies, which are mostly insects such as some beetles, sawflies, and weevils that are found in Asia, did not come to the United States with it. Without these **predators**, there was nothing to control the growth of the vine.

In the 1950s, the government's **perspective** on kudzu began to change. People were beginning to discover that kudzu wasn't a miracle vine after all. In fact, there were actually huge **disadvantages** to growing it.

Kudzu does help to prevent soil erosion. However, as it cures that particular problem, it creates other problems. Kudzu is such a **robust** plant that it just keeps on growing and growing. It will cover chicken coops, barns, garages, chimneys, mailboxes, and houses—anything! Entire buildings covered with kudzu are common sights in the South today. Kudzu will cover abandoned cars, trucks, and farm equipment. It can take over entire fields. It grows well in cities, too, and will even grow in the middle of parking lots.

In some places, kudzu was planted along highways to stop soil erosion. However, it also grows over highway signs, creating a **predicament** for drivers—they can't read the signs! It also climbs utility poles. Sometimes, it causes electrical shorts that lead to power failures.

By the year 1953, the U.S. government had changed its mind about kudzu and had stopped encouraging people to grow it. In 1972, the U.S. Department of Agriculture declared kudzu to be a weed. However, by then, kudzu was well on its way to "eating" the South.

Weevils help control the growth of kudzu in Asia.

Kudzu Spreads Its Tentacles

Kudzu also causes **formidable** problems for other living things. It can cover entire trees, blocking the sunlight from reaching them. Without sunlight, the trees will eventually die. If many trees die, an entire forest might be lost.

In addition, kudzu has very heavy roots. A vine that has been growing for 20 years can weigh 250 pounds or more. Some kudzu roots weigh as much as 400 pounds. When a kudzu vine completely grows over a tree, the weight of its roots pulls on the tree. If the roots are too heavy, the tree trunk may break under all that weight. The tree's survival may even be threatened. One scientist working for the U.S. Forest Service has said that he has seen kudzu pull down an entire tree!

Kudzu's ability to grow so fast has earned it many nicknames. In addition to being called the vine that ate the South, it's also called the mile-a-minute vine and foot-a-night vine. Some people in the South joke that they have to close their windows at night to keep kudzu out of their house. Yet this isn't always a joke.

Today, kudzu covers more than 7 million acres of the South. That amount of space is the same as if the entire state of Massachusetts were covered with kudzu! The plant is most abundant in Alabama, Georgia, North Carolina, South Carolina, and Mississippi.

Unfortunately, kudzu is spreading. It now grows as far north as Massachusetts and as far west as Texas. It has even been found in Oregon. In colder climates, it doesn't grow as well as it does in the South. However, the fact that it's managed to move so far shows how easily it can adapt to a new environment.

Kudzu can become an even greater problem than it is now. What can we do about it? How can we stop this **apparently** unstoppable vine from "eating" the rest of the South and then continuing on across the country? Solving this problem is more of a challenge than you might think.

Some people have tried to pull the vines completely out of the ground, but that can't always be easily done. Can you imagine trying to tear out a root system that weighs more than 250 pounds? In some places, heavy earth-moving equipment might be required to eliminate the vast amounts of kudzu.

Scientists have tried to get rid of kudzu using herbicides. However, they have found that kudzu is able to resist most chemicals that are commonly used to kill plants. Even the strongest of herbicides can take many years to kill larger kudzu plants. Some herbicides have little or no effect on kudzu. One type, claims a scientist, even makes this stubborn vine grow better!

A mighty root system hides beneath the kudzu vine.

17

Kudzu—Foe and Friend?

There are some insect species in the United States that eat kudzu seeds. Unfortunately, kudzu's main way of spreading isn't from its seeds but from its roots. U.S. scientists are trying to learn more about kudzu's natural enemies in China. One **predator** is a large beetle that feeds on kudzu roots. This beetle isn't found in the United States, so why not just bring it here and let it eat the kudzu? Well, that would be an intentional introduction. Remember—that's what brought kudzu here in the first place! Before we bring in a beetle to eat kudzu, we have to know what else the beetle might eat and how else it might **interact** with its new environment. If this beetle eats kudzu but also eats other important plants or crops and has no natural enemies in the South, we'd be creating a whole new problem!

Here is another example of unintentional introduction. People often spread kudzu as they build roads and put up buildings. It's very common for people to unknowingly carry a kudzu root from one place to another as they move building supplies or soil.

Is there nothing we can do to halt this invading vine, then? In fact, there may be a very simple answer: goats. Goats have very **robust** appetites. They'll eat just about anything, and they like munching on kudzu.

Scientists have found that goats can stop an entire field of kudzu from growing. If the goats are left in the field long enough, they will eat all of the kudzu!

However, before we turn thousands of goats loose to graze away all the kudzu, we should consider this: We may not want to completely get rid of kudzu. In Asia, people have found many uses for it. They make food from kudzu's starchy roots and use its vines to make paper. For thousands of years they've been using kudzu root as a medicine.

In the United States, some people use the kudzu vine to make baskets and paper. Others make tea from kudzu leaves, or they make jelly and syrup from the blossoms. Also, research is being done to see if kudzu can be used to help treat alcoholism. From this viewpoint, kudzu has **economic** and social value.

Perhaps, then, the real answer is not to completely eliminate kudzu but to control it so that it helps us instead of attacks us. If we can do that, kudzu might change from being an invader to being an ally.

The kudzu vine grows about a foot a day. At this rate, it won't be long before these ruins are completely covered.

CHAPTER 4

A Strange Silence

Brown tree snake

Guam is an island in the Pacific Ocean. A territory of the United States, Guam is about 1,500 miles southeast of Tokyo, Japan, and part of a group of islands called the Mariana Islands. Guam is the largest of these islands and the farthest south. It's about 212 square miles, or slightly smaller than the city of Chicago.

If you visited this tropical island about 50 years ago, you would have heard several species of birds singing in its thick forests. Today, the forests are strangely quiet, what one person has called an "eerie silence." You may be wondering how this change is possible. Guam is silent because there are very few birds left on the island. What happened to them? That's a frequently asked question. The answer is the brown tree snake.

The brown tree snake is native to some other islands in the Pacific. It can grow as long as 8 feet and weigh up to 5 pounds. Because it is a nocturnal animal, the brown tree snake is active mostly during the night.

Brown tree snakes have a highly developed sense of smell. They can also see very well in the dark. These abilities are especially helpful for finding prey at night. Brown tree snakes feed on the eggs of birds and reptiles and small mammals.

Brown tree snakes may reproduce as often as twice a year. The female releases up to 12 leathery eggs at a time. She leaves them in places such as hollow trees and caves where they won't dry out from the heat. After depositing her eggs, the female slithers away and abandons them. The young snakes hatch about 90 days later. When they're born, they're about 18 inches in length. By the time they are about a year old, they can reach lengths of 3 feet or more.

The brown tree snake is mildly poisonous. It kills its prey by first biting it. The snake's poison, or venom, is then released as it chews on its prey. This venom doesn't usually kill people, but it can make babies and small children very sick.

In addition to using venom on its prey, the brown tree snake wraps its powerful body around its victim. This action holds the prey in place while the snake bites into it. Unlike some large snakes that strangle prey (such as the boa constrictor and anaconda), the brown tree snake can't strangle adult humans. However, it can harm young children.

As you would expect from a snake that lives in trees, the brown tree snake is an excellent climber. Unfortunately for people, it doesn't stay in trees. It often moves into homes, offices, stores, and other buildings, looking for food and a place to hide during daytime.

A brown tree snake will hide just about anywhere that gives it shelter from bright light. It also doesn't like high temperatures. Its ability to coil into a tight ball enables it to squeeze into extremely small spaces.

The Invader Arrives

It is believed that the brown tree snake arrived on Guam from New Guinea, which is about 800 miles away. How did it cross hundreds of miles of ocean to get to Guam?

During World War II, there was a lot of fighting on many Pacific islands. Military planes were flying from island to island, and warships were carrying soldiers and supplies all around the Pacific.

Wildlife experts think that the brown tree snake arrived on Guam in the late 1940s, unnoticed on military planes or cargo ships coming from New Guinea. The first sightings of the snake on Guam were in the early 1950s. By the early 1960s, the snakes were very common in central Guam. Toward the end of the 1960s, they were being seen all around the island.

At the same time the snakes were spreading all around Guam, something else was happening on the island—birds were disappearing. In the 1960s, wildlife experts noticed that there were no longer any birds on a third of the southern tip of the island. They also noticed that the areas in which the birds were disappearing were slowly extending north. By the end of the 1970s, there were no longer any birds on two-thirds of southern Guam. By the middle of the 1980s, the only places where birds could be found were in small areas on the northern end of the island. In addition, many species of birds that were native to Guam were gone entirely.

Some people believed that a pesticide sprayed on the island during an organized attempt to kill mosquitoes had killed the birds. Other people thought the birds were dying from a disease. However, a biologist named Julie Savidge had a different idea. She realized that Guam's birds were disappearing in an **evolving** pattern that exactly matched the spread of the brown tree snake across Guam. The snake was spreading from south to north. The birds were disappearing from south to north. Brown tree snakes were **apparently** killing the birds.

On Guam, the brown tree snake had found the perfect **circumstances** in which to thrive. It had very few natural enemies, and there was plenty of prey. With such a large food supply and so few **predators**, the brown tree snake population increased enormously. Today, in some parts of Guam, there are as many as 13,000 snakes per square mile!

Brown tree snakes are arboreal. This means they live mainly in trees. However, they hunt for food both in trees and on the ground.

Can This Invader Be Stopped?

The brown tree snake has entirely wiped out several native bird species on Guam. In fact, birds have nearly vanished from the island's forests. Some of these species of birds may not be found anywhere else in the world. If so, these species are now extinct, like the dinosaurs. Several other species of birds native to Guam are near extinction.

The brown tree snake has also become a **formidable** threat to other animals on Guam. Just as many birds have disappeared from the island, so have some species of native lizards. Guam once had 12 kinds of native lizards. Today, most have disappeared from the island. Guam once had three species of native bat. Today, only one species still remains.

The brown tree snake isn't a threat only in the wild. Its **interactions** with people have caused serious problems. It has also hurt Guam's **economy**. For example, the snakes crawling on electrical wires can cause power failures. Between 1978 and 1997, more than 1,600 power failures occurred because of these snakes. Power failures cause food to spoil and computers to malfunction. Traffic lights stop working, causing accidents. Equipment has to be repaired. In this way alone, the brown tree snake costs Guam millions of dollars in damages every year.

After one major power failure, it was reported that a brown tree snake had tried to eat a baby pigeon in a nest on a power pole. According to the report, during the struggle the snake **apparently** came into contact with an electrical conductor. There was an electrical surge that caused the power failure. Most power failures caused by brown tree snakes aren't widespread. Yet even small power failures show how much trouble the brown tree snake causes the people of Guam.

The brown tree snake is a problem for people in other ways, too. For example, it is an aggressive snake. Instead of running away when it feels threatened, it will attack.

The brown tree snake doesn't seem to be afraid of people. It will enter areas where there is lots of human activity. It invades farms and often goes into poultry houses to eat chickens and chicken eggs. It will crawl into people's yards and attack pets. It will even go into people's homes, and if it encounters people there, it is likely to bite. Its most common victims are sleeping babies less than six months old.

In dealing with the brown tree snake, the people of Guam are wrestling with two related **predicaments**. The first is how to control this fierce invader. As with other invasive species, getting rid of the brown tree snake can often seem to be an impossible task.

The brown tree snake is spreading from Guam to the other Pacific islands (highlighted in red) on this map.

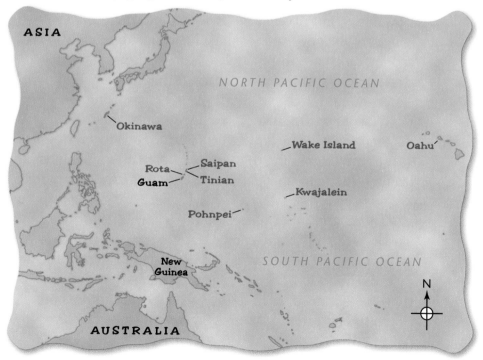

People who deliberately kill the brown tree snakes or accidentally run over them in cars eliminate a large number of the snakes every year. Snakes are also electrocuted as they climb on power lines. Pigs and monitor lizards like to eat brown tree snakes. However, not enough brown tree snakes die in these ways to keep the population in check.

Chemicals, poisons, and traps are being tried, but so far nothing has worked very well. Now, however, there may be some hope, from something as simple as a product most people have in their medicine cabinets at home—the pain reliever and fever reducer acetaminophen. Scientists have been putting acetaminophen into dead mice and leaving the mice out for the snakes to eat. Although most snakes don't eat dead animals, brown tree snakes do. When the snakes eat the mice, the acetaminophen kills the snakes. Perhaps the problem of controlling the snake population on Guam will soon be solved.

The second **predicament** with the brown tree snake is how to keep it from leaving Guam. Just as easily as it arrived on Guam from a distant island, it can leave Guam and travel to other places. If that happened, the same situation that has **evolved** on Guam would very likely occur to wherever else the snake traveled.

As part of a constant effort to keep the brown tree snake from spreading to other places, planes and ships leaving Guam are inspected regularly to make sure there are no brown tree snakes aboard. There are snake traps at airports and other places on the island. Authorities use dogs to sniff planes and cargo for snakes. In addition, when planes and ships from Guam arrive at their destinations, they're inspected again to see if any snakes were missed. These steps enable authorities on Guam to capture thousands of snakes each year.

Even so, brown tree snakes can be **elusive** in hiding from authorities and leaving Guam. They have been found on other islands in the Mariana group, including Saipan, Tinian, and Rota. They've also been discovered on other Pacific islands, such as Kwajalein, Wake, Pohnpei, and Oahu. In addition, the brown tree snake has been found on islands much farther away, such as Diego Garcia in the Indian Ocean and the Japanese island of Okinawa. In 1993, a brown tree snake was even found in Corpus Christi, Texas. So far, the brown tree snake has not established itself in any of these places the way it has on Guam. However, in Saipan, its population is definitely increasing.

The most common way for a brown tree snake to move from one place to another is by airplane. It will crawl up a wheel of a grounded airplane, then coil up inside the wheel well. A wheel well is the part of the airplane into which a wheel is raised once the plane is in the air. If the snake is not discovered before a plane takes off, the snake will crawl back down the wheel and slither away to its new habitat once the plane has landed.

An Unusual Story

Some people who study snakes have said that the story of the brown tree snake is unusual. They believe this is the first and perhaps only example of a snake being responsible for the extinction of other species. They say it's usually the other way around. When an invading species arrives in a new habitat, snakes are often the ones eaten by the new species. However, on Guam, the brown tree snake has definitely taken control.

The coqui frog performs its nighttime chant.

CHAPTER 5
Deafening Frogs

Imagine that you are in Hawaii. It is a lovely evening, and you are attending an outdoor theater presentation. The breezes are blowing gently around you. The musicians are tuning their instruments. **Apparently**, the show is about to begin.

The actors come out on the stage. You sit back to enjoy the show. The actors are speaking and **interacting** with each other. However, you are having trouble hearing them. As you look around the audience, you notice other people having the same problem. Strange noises, you realize, are coming from the gardens near the theater. Is it birds chirping? The loud, screeching sounds increase. You cannot believe your ears. It sounds like a pack of banshees on the loose. Then, you realize that you are hearing a nighttime chorus of alien invaders—coqui frogs.

Hawaii is a land of plentiful vegetation. The warm temperatures and high humidity make Hawaii an ideal new home for many alien invaders. More than 1,000 alien plants and animals from all over the world have been introduced by accident to Hawaii. The invading species become quite at home. Some of these species are more welcome than others.

Little Frog, Big Problems

One of these unwelcome species was introduced to Hawaii in about 1988. Called the coqui (scientific name, *Eleutherodactylus*), this frog may be green, yellowish-green, light brown, or dark brown. The coqui has varying patterns on its skin, including a light stripe that runs down the middle of its back. Adult coquis measure up to 2 inches in length. Not swimmers, coquis have disks or pads on the tips of their toes. These pads help them adhere to surfaces such as moist leaves.

Coquis have an unusual reproduction cycle. There is no tadpole stage. Tiny, but fully formed, froglets emerge from the eggs. The coqui has a tiny tail when it is born that soon disappears. A female coqui can lay up to 6 clutches of eggs per year, with an average of 28 eggs per clutch.

The population of coqui frogs in Hawaii keeps growing, partly because the coqui has few natural **predators** there. Another reason for the coquis' success in Hawaii is that the babies, unlike tadpoles, don't need a body of water in which to hatch from their eggs. Just one pair of coqui can have 10,000 descendants in 1 year!

Coqui frogs are nocturnal. That means they are active at night. Their chirping can be heard most often beginning at sunset and continuing on through the night.

They also can be heard during rainy downpours. The male coquis are the real noisemakers. Their mating sound is a loud "Ko-KEE," giving them their name. The females and young make few sounds.

The coqui is native to Puerto Rico and the southeastern United States, particularly Florida. Scientists think that the frogs probably arrived in Hawaii in potted plants that came from Florida or Puerto Rico. The frogs then moved from plant nurseries to home gardens and woodlands, where they thrived.

The coqui frog is a serious threat to Hawaii for many reasons. The frog preys on native insects, spiders, and snails. Scientists have calculated that each day these frog **predators** can eat as many as 114,000 insects! That might sound like a good thing. However, those insects are also food for native Hawaiian birds. Many native forest birds are already in decline. If the birds have to compete with the tiny frogs for food, more birds may die.

Although coqui frogs are insect eaters, they usually prefer crawling bugs and spiders. **Robust** colonies of coqui can eat up to 200 pounds of bugs per acre each year. The Hawaiian agriculture actually depends on its bug population to keep the special ecology of the region intact. The Department of Agriculture (DOA) has designated the coqui as an agricultural pest. This designation makes it illegal to ship the frogs within the state and to release them deliberately. However, it is still not legal to exterminate coqui on private property without the owner's permission. The DOA might have to take action soon, to better regulate the exploding coqui populations.

The tiny coqui frog has a huge appetite and a surprisingly noisy screech.

Besides causing problems to Hawaii's environment, coqui frogs create a major noise nuisance. A noise nuisance may not seem like such a big deal. However, it is. For one thing, the loud screeching sounds of a group of these frogs at night can be truly disturbing. The sounds can even prevent people from getting the sleep that is **vital** to their health.

The tourist industry is very important to the **economy** of Hawaii. If the coqui frog population spreads to hotel and resort grounds, disturbing guests and damaging the environment, it would create a major **disadvantage** for this industry. Owners of businesses connected with tourism are concerned that the coqui will hurt tourism and their businesses.

Officials in Hawaii have tried various ways to control the coqui frog population. One approach was to use a very hot water bath on plants used for landscaping. The water drives off the frogs hiding in the plants, and they can be captured more easily. However, if areas are heavily infested with coquis, or if hot water is not readily available, this method will not be very effective.

Other substances have been tried as ways to cut down on the coqui population. One approach was to use a caffeine spray. The solution killed the frogs, but it may have been harmful to water quality. Citric acid has also been effective in killing the frogs as well as their eggs. However, the citric acid is harmful to some sensitive plants. Nursery owners are reluctant to make use of citric acid for this reason.

Other methods of controlling this frog are being explored, and educational materials are being distributed to homeowners. These materials can help homeowners identify the coquis and learn how to discourage the tiny, noisy creatures from taking up residence in their yards.

Zebra mussels

CHAPTER 6
The Mussel With Muscle

It's the mid to late 1980s. The place is the Great Lakes region of the United States. A ship is arriving from Europe. Perhaps it is in one of the smaller lakes in the area, such as Lake St. Clair. A stowaway is on board the ship, a shellfish from Europe. Within a few years this shellfish would become one of the Great Lakes region's most **formidable** invaders: the zebra mussel.

Many ocean vessels carry seawater, called ballast water, to help balance the boat. When the ship no longer needs the extra water for balance, the ballast tanks are emptied into whatever waters the ship is in. In the 1980s, when a ship's ballast tanks were emptied into the Great Lakes region, the mussels must have unknowingly been set loose.

Zebra mussels are mollusks. The mollusk group includes the octopus, squid, snail, and slug. Mussels are "bivalves." That means they have two shells, or valves. Other bivalves are clams, oysters, and scallops. Many bivalves are edible and are important food items. One bivalve, the oyster, gives us pearls.

The zebra mussel gets its name from the dark stripes on its shells. Zebra mussels are not very big—generally about 1 inch long. Some grow as big as 2 inches. Zebra mussels **sustain** themselves by eating tiny algae and plankton, which are small organisms that live in the water.

Although mussels live in water, they don't swim. Instead, they attach themselves to objects or other sea creatures. Sometimes huge clusters of zebra mussels attach themselves to the same thing.

Zebra mussels reproduce very rapidly. Females generally begin reproducing when they are 2 years old. They can produce more than 40,000 eggs in one reproductive cycle, and up to 1 million eggs in one spawning season. Zebra mussels generally live for about 4 to 5 years. So even if a female zebra mussel lays eggs for only 2 years, she can produce as many as 2 million eggs.

About 3 to 5 days after the eggs are fertilized, the babies, or larvae, emerge. Newborn zebra mussels are called veligers. For about a month, they drift in water, carried along by the current. Then, they settle on the bottom, where they crawl about, searching for something to which they can attach themselves.

Some mussels live in the ocean. Zebra mussels are freshwater mussels, which means they live in rivers and lakes. They're native to rivers and lakes in eastern Europe and western Asia. Their habitats included the Caspian Sea, bordering Russia, and the Ural River in Russia. By the early 1900s, zebra mussels had spread throughout Europe by attaching themselves to ship bottoms.

The zebra mussel was found in Lake St. Clair in the Great Lakes region in 1988. Because it had few natural enemies in North America, it thrived in the waters of these huge lakes. However, it did more than thrive. Like the brown tree snake and the kudzu vine, it began to **impose** itself on its new habitat.

The zebra mussel has had a major impact on the waters of the Great Lakes. For example, it has been slowly killing off many other species of mussels. It does this partly by feeding on the food that these mussels eat.

The zebra mussel eats enormous amounts of algae and phytoplankton (tiny plants that float in water). In the Great Lakes, it has greatly reduced the food supplies of the native mussels. Deprived of their food, the native mussels have begun to die off. Most native species of mussel have now almost disappeared from Lake St. Clair and from the western basin of Lake Erie.

The zebra mussel has harmed native mussel species in yet another way. Sometimes whole colonies of zebra mussels have attached themselves to native mussels. This behavior makes it hard—and can even make it impossible—for the other mussels to function. As many as 10,000 zebra mussels have attached themselves to a single native mussel at one time.

By disrupting the food chain in its new habitat, the zebra mussel has also affected other native organisms. Mussels eat by taking in water and filtering it to remove the algae. In the Great Lakes, zebra mussels are filtering huge amounts of water. This

What kind of problem do mussels cause when they cluster in pipes?

has made the water appear very clear, which makes some people think the lakes have gotten cleaner. In filtering out the algae in the water, they're taking food from native organisms that eat algae.

In addition, by eating so much phytoplankton, zebra mussels are also taking food away from small fish. Without food, these fish die, which means there is less food for bigger fish. As this pattern develops, the habitat contains less and less food and cannot **sustain** as many species as it once did. In this way, the zebra mussel is **imposing** hardships on much of the wildlife that depends on the Great Lakes for food.

Zebra mussels are also causing an enormous amount of **economic** damage. Huge numbers of mussels attach themselves to the water supply pipes of factories, public water pumping stations, water treatment facilities, and power plants. They clog the pipes until the water stops flowing. They also clog air conditioning systems, cooling systems, and fire fighting equipment. Power plants and other facilities that use lake and river water spend millions of dollars to detect and remove zebra mussels.

When enough zebra mussels attach themselves to the bottom of a boat, the boat can be harder to steer. A boat that is hard to steer can become a safety hazard. In addition, small mussels clog the cooling systems of boat engines, causing the engines to overheat. Zebra mussels also attach themselves to buoys, which are floating objects used for navigation. Some buoys have had so many zebra mussels on them that they sank! Dealing with all the problems **imposed** by zebra mussels costs millions of dollars every year.

These problems would be bad enough if the zebra mussel were only in the Great Lakes. However, zebra mussels are spreading to other bodies of water. They're in many of the large rivers of the Midwest, including the Mississippi, Ohio, Tennessee, Arkansas, Illinois, and Cumberland rivers. They're in the Hudson River, in New York. Zebra mussels or their larvae have been found in Nebraska, Kansas, and Virginia. Wildlife experts think that zebra mussels are already in hundreds of U.S. lakes and could someday spread to most bodies of fresh water in the United States.

How are they spreading? In most cases, people spread them. In many rivers where zebra mussels are appearing, there is a lot of barge traffic. In other places, there are many small fishing boats and recreational boats. As we saw, zebra mussels will attach themselves to the bottom of a boat in one river or lake, and fall off the boat or be scraped off in another location. With few or no natural enemies and their fast reproduction, zebra mussels soon establish themselves in a new habitat.

People spread zebra mussels in other ways, too. The mussel larvae are too small to be seen by people. Because the larvae are so small, they can easily travel in water carried by boats. Fishing boats usually carry water in which to put fish that are caught. People who fish often carry bait buckets containing water. Zebra mussel larvae can travel in this water and be taken from one lake or river to another. Zebra mussel larvae can even travel on SCUBA equipment.

Zebra mussels can live outside of water for several days if the temperature is not too hot. As a result, they can travel attached to boats being towed on a trailer from one body of water to another. In this way, zebra mussels can travel overland from state to state.

So how do we stop zebra mussels from spreading? What can be done to eliminate them from bodies of water they've already invaded? Many things have been tried, including freezing them and using steam, electricity, and sound to try to kill them. However, by now you know how difficult it can be to get rid of an invasive species. Natural methods, such as introducing **predators**, parasites, and diseases, mean introducing yet another nonnative species. As we've clearly seen, when we do that, we can't always accurately predict what will happen next.

Some birds will eat zebra mussels. You might think that would help reduce the mussel population, right? Zebra mussels, however, can even pose a threat to birds and other **predators**.

Look at how many zebra mussels are on this shopping cart that ended up underwater.

As zebra mussels filter water, they absorb dangerous chemicals and store them in their bodies. Birds that eat zebra mussels can die from these poisons. Many Great Lakes birds that ate the mussels have died.

Another **predator** that eats zebra mussels is a fish called the round goby. When gobies eat zebra mussels, their bodies absorb poisons from the mussels. Higher in the food chain, birds such as loons and gulls eat round gobies. When the birds eat the poisoned gobies, the birds die. Thousands of water birds have been found dead on the shores of the Great Lakes.

The zebra mussel has become such a big problem that it is monitored constantly. On the Internet, Web sites have maps that show the latest sightings of zebra mussels. The war against these mussels has been extremely frustrating. If we are fortunate, a weapon will soon **evolve** that turns the tide against the tiny but tough zebra mussel.

Zebra mussels have spread from the Great Lakes to other waters as shown on this map.

What Can We Do?

Invasive species come in many sizes, shapes, and forms. Scientists estimate that in the United States alone, there are about 50,000 nonnative species. This estimate includes those that are helpful as well as those that are threats.

Some invaders are not even living organisms. Each winter, people worry about catching the flu. Yet a virus that usually starts in Asia causes the flu. To the rest of the world, this virus is an invader.

One study has shown that in the United States alone, invading species have cost the **economy** more than $138 billion every year in ruined property and loss of resources. By some estimates, this cost is higher than for all other natural disasters combined!

Scientists are working hard to stop invasive species from causing more damage, and everyone can help. Owners of **exotic** pets should never turn them loose in the wild. That's how those snakehead fish got into that pond in Maryland. People should not try to sneak **exotic** plants into places where they are not legal. Boat owners should inspect and clean their boats regularly to make sure there are no invaders such as zebra mussels attached. People who fish should not empty their bait buckets into new bodies of water.

These safety measures won't solve all our invasive species problems, of course. However, they could stop a species from invading a habitat. They might prevent an invader that's already there from spreading to a new habitat.

As we've seen, alien invaders don't have to come from space to be frightening. Where will the next big threat come from? No one knows. You can bet, however, that it's out there, lurking in the shadows, waiting for just the right moment to take control.

EPIDEMIC!

by Lilly Golden

CHAPTER 1
Plagues
AND Pandemics

Did you ever wonder how and why people get sick? How can you feel just fine one day and awful the next?

About 100 years ago, some scientists created a theory to explain why people get sick. Called the germ theory, it was the most important contribution made to the field of medicine. The theory suggested that tiny bodies (germs) cause illnesses. Germs are so tiny that they can only be seen using high-powered microscopes. Imagine things so small that they cannot be seen by the naked eye having such a huge effect on people.

Before the germ theory, there was a **profusion** of other theories. Some people blamed illnesses on the positions of planets and stars or on something they called miasma, which means "bad air." Once the germ theory was accepted, people began to understand more about the process of disease.

Early scientists noticed that some diseases could be spread from one person to another. When a disease affects many people in an area, it is known as an epidemic. If it spreads to other countries and continents, it is called a pandemic. A particularly deadly epidemic or pandemic is referred to as a plague.

In this painting, disease is shown as a deadly warrior.

Some germs exist in our bodies without making us sick. Others can cause us harm. Some germs attack the body **externally**, such as a rash on the skin. Other germs attack the body internally, as in the common cold, causing **congestion** in the nose or chest.

Germs that cause illnesses can be bacteria or viruses. If the germ is a type of bacteria, an infected person can usually be given medicines to fight the infection. These medicines, called antibiotics, were first developed in 1940. Before then, bacterial infections were often fatal.

If the germ that causes an illness is a virus, medical treatment is often **futile**. However, the body's immune system produces special proteins called antibodies that can usually fight off illnesses caused by viruses.

Imagine bacteria or viruses as creatures that live inside the body, feasting on it, like parasites. The body is the host. Because the germs may eventually kill their host, they must find somewhere else to live before the host dies. Bacteria and viruses have developed ways of spreading from host to host so they can survive and reproduce **indefinitely**.

Colds and the flu spread easily from person to person. The viruses that cause them travel through the air. What if a virus is a killer? What if that killer virus is very contagious and is spread through the air? There could be an epidemic or even a pandemic. With the popularity of air travel today, people can easily travel from place to place. A frequently moving person can take a deadly illness into another country in just a few hours.

In the pages that follow, you will learn about some epidemics and pandemics, including a plague called the Black Death and the flu of 1918. You will also read about deadly diseases, such as smallpox and cholera, that have been cured by modern medicine. Finally, you will learn about some of the epidemics and pandemics that continue to challenge medical professionals today.

CHAPTER 2
The Black Death

In 1347, a ship pulled into a harbor in Messina, Italy, with dying men at the oars. The men stumbled off the ship. They had **grotesque** swellings (called buboes) the size of eggs or apples under their arms and on their groins. These swellings oozed blood and pus.

The men's skin was covered with boils and black blotches that were caused by internal bleeding. The victims smelled awful, and everything that came out of their bodies was bloody. They suffered terrible pain and most died within 5 days of their arrival. The disease was bubonic plague, or the plague. The plague spread death throughout Europe. Because of the black blotches, people often referred to the plague as the Black Death.

Although people who lived during the fourteenth century did not know it, the plague was caused by bacteria. When bacteria infected a person, that person became ill within 2 to 6 days. Once stricken, few people recovered.

Citizens load a plague victim onto a wagon.

Within 100 years of its introduction into Europe, the plague had killed one-third of the population of the continent. The people of the fourteenth century thought the world was coming to an end.

In rural areas, farmers collapsed in their fields. Crops failed. Cows, horses, goats, and pigs wandered off or died from hunger. In some cities, bubonic plague killed nearly everyone. The number of people who died was staggering. Graveyards quickly filled up. After a while, there was no more room to bury the growing numbers of dead bodies. Those people who were still living began dumping the dead bodies in huge pits that soon overflowed.

Dead family members were buried quickly in shallow graves. Sometimes dogs would find these graves, drag out the corpses, and eat them. Bodies were stacked in the streets because there was no one left to pick them up.

People suspected that the disease was somehow spread by contact. They feared getting close to anyone who was sick with the plague, even if that person was a friend, a brother, a mother, or a child.

How did people cope with so much sickness and death around them? The rules of society began to break down. Fathers and mothers abandoned sick children. Children ran away from parents. Neighbor avoided neighbor. People knew by the stench coming from a house nearby that the residents inside had died.

Some people seemed to feel that obeying laws was pointless. They spent their days stealing and partying. They wasted all their money and food. Others decided to escape from their stricken cities to the country. They **futilely** believed that by living quietly they could escape the dreaded plague.

Yet it didn't matter where or how people lived. The plague visited city and countryside. It struck the rich as well as the poor. The plague killed young and old alike.

How Was the Plague Spread?

People of the fourteenth century did not understand how disease spread. They did not know much about effective methods of **prevention**. They did not realize that the carriers of the plague were right under their noses—rats and their **accompanying** fleas.

Living conditions in the fourteenth century were quite different from those of today. People were so used to living with rats and fleas that they barely noticed them. Farm animals lived in the homes with people, and garbage and sewage filled the streets. People rarely bathed, and their clothes were covered with lice and fleas.

People had no idea what caused the plague. In addition, people didn't know anything about the germ theory. Yet, of course, everyone wanted to be spared from the deadly disease. So people tried many different ways to fight off the disease or to protect themselves. For example, some people dipped handkerchiefs in strong-smelling oils, thinking the oils would ward off sickness. Some thought that keeping dead animals in their homes would prevent them from getting sick. Others placed dead toads on the buboes to absorb the poison. Some people even beat themselves with sticks.

Of course, nothing people did to ward off the plague worked. The real villains of the plague were the bacteria that lived on the fleas. The fleas lived on the rats but often jumped onto people. Nearly everyone who was bitten by an infected flea became infected with the plague.

What caused the plague? Fleas were a part of the problem.

45

The bubonic plague first occurred in China in about 1330. Flea-infested rats hid aboard ships and carried the disease from port to port, spreading it throughout Asia and Europe. As the disease continued to spread, it changed in nature. Instead of there being **external** signs, such as swellings, people had very high fevers and began coughing. This form of the plague was even deadlier than the first. The victims coughed up frothy blood and died within several days or even sooner— sometimes in less than 24 hours. Some doctors died at the bedsides of their patients. A person might even go to bed well and die in his or her sleep.

This second form of the disease was called pneumonic plague. Pneumonic plague was spread through the air. No one was safe.

The Plague Dies Down

By the end of the fourteenth century, the plague had subsided, though people of the time must have thought it would go on **indefinitely**. It is estimated that between 20 million and 40 million people died during the time of the Black Death.

However, the plague did not disappear altogether. Even today, bubonic plague lives on, and every few years there is an outbreak that affects a few thousand people. The most recent **recurrence** was in India in 1994, where 2,500 people came down with the plague. As recently as 1999, a 13-year-old boy in Kazakhstan, a country near Russia, died of bubonic plague.

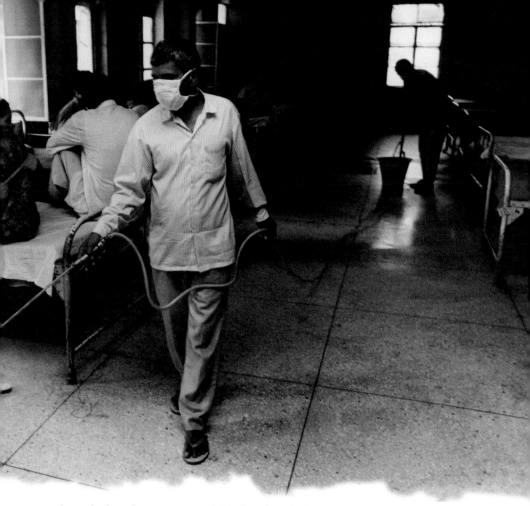

A masked worker sprays pesticide in a hospital in New Delhi, India.

The plague lives on in the United States, too. The states of New Mexico, Arizona, Colorado, and California see the most cases of plague because of the presence of the animals that carry the bacteria. In 1996, two Americans died of the plague. They had gotten it from fleas that had jumped from prairie dogs onto them. However, the number of cases is incredibly low—from 10 to 20 cases per year. Today, by keeping populations of rats and other rodents that carry fleas under control, the risk of getting the plague is low.

Plague Prevention

The best method of **preventing** the plague from being passed on to people is rat or flea control. However, cats can get pneumonic plague, and people can catch it by breathing airborne droplets from a cat's sneeze.

The bubonic plague has a mortality rate of between 60 percent and 75 percent. A mortality rate of 75 percent means that if 100 people come down with a disease and aren't treated, only about 25 of them will live. Pneumonic plague has nearly a 100 percent mortality rate. This rate means that every person who is infected will die unless he or she gets to a hospital immediately.

Efforts are underway to create a vaccine for the plague. Vaccines are injections or oral medicines that help us form our own antibodies to fight infection. People who are at high risk, that is, those most likely to be exposed to the disease, would be able to get the vaccine.

Fortunately, today, there are antibiotics for treating plague. A person exposed to the disease, say, by coming in contact with an infected flea, can be treated. Antibiotic treatment, given quickly, is effective. The **outlook** for someone treated with antibiotic drugs is good. If not for antibiotics, plague would be just as deadly today as it was long ago.

Protective clothing at the time of the Black Death

48

CHAPTER 3
Smallpox

Smallpox is one of the most feared diseases of all time. Over the course of history, it has killed millions of people. In the twentieth century alone, more than 300 million people died from smallpox.

Smallpox is a highly contagious disease that is caused by the variola virus. If the virus spreads to a person's organs, it can lead to death. The first symptoms of smallpox are a high fever (from 102°F to 105°F) and terrible pains in the head, back, and stomach.

A few days later, tiny red dots become **visible** in the mouth and throat. These dots develop into sores that break open. At this point, the victim is very contagious. Next, a rash begins on the forehead. This rash spreads to the whole face, then to the body, and last, to the arms, legs, hands, and feet. The rash becomes raised, and each bump fills with fluid. The bumps become hard, as if peas were buried under the skin. Finally, crusty scabs form over the bumps. The victim is a **grotesque** mass of scabs and is contagious until the last scab falls off the body. Scars from smallpox are deep and permanent.

Smallpox, also known as variola, comes in two basic types: variola major and variola minor. Variola minor is a mild form of the disease and is rarely fatal. Variola major is much more dangerous and is the more common type.

Smallpox has existed for more than 3,000 years. The earliest known case of smallpox was found on the mummified body of Pharaoh Ramses V of Egypt, who died in 1157 BCE. Small scars covering the pharaoh's body were evidence of the disease.

Smallpox spread throughout the world. It reached Europe more than 2,500 years ago and continued its march. It reached Australia last of all in the 1700s.

How does smallpox spread? You catch smallpox by touching the skin lesions, clothing, or bedding of a person with an active case and sometimes just by breathing the same air. It takes about 2 weeks to get sick after coming into contact with variola. During that time, the virus is multiplying and traveling around the body through the bloodstream.

The smallpox virus has caused sickness and death for thousands of years. How does the disease reach a population that has not been affected previously? The native people of the early Americas offer a good example of how a disease can take hold where it has not been before.

Destruction of the Native Americans

The native peoples of the Americas had lived for thousands of years untroubled by some of the worst diseases known to affect humankind. They had never been exposed to the plague and many other illnesses that people of Europe had suffered from for centuries.

This illustration from the sixteenth century shows an Aztec medicine man treating a smallpox victim during an epidemic in Mexico.

When ships from Europe landed on the shores of the Americas, they brought with them horses, guns, and something even more destructive than guns—smallpox. Not a single Native American had immunity to this disease. The contagious smallpox virus rapidly spread from person to person. In some areas, 95 percent of a group was killed. In others, every man, woman, and child perished.

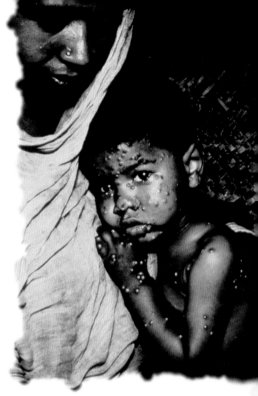

A smallpox victim

The Native Americans quickly learned that in order to survive the disease they had to avoid exposure to it. As a result, many victims were left alone in agony, without anyone to get them food or water.

So many died that no one remained to bury the corpses, and crows and wolves feasted on them where they lay. Colonists who arrived a few years later found no living people, only piles of skulls and bones.

Is there any good news? If a victim survives, which there is a one-in-three chance of doing, he or she will never get smallpox again. Once a person has had smallpox, that person has immunity. Immunity means the person has protection. Like some other viruses, including measles, the disease will never **recur**. You can't get smallpox twice.

What is even better news? Smallpox is no longer a major threat. It is believed to have been completely wiped out by 1980. A vaccine was developed that successfully ended the spread of smallpox.

Fighting Back

Long before vaccinations had been developed, in some parts of the world, doctors used a **preventive** medical technique called variolation. They took pus from the pox and injected it under the skin of a healthy person. That person would then get only a mild case of smallpox.

Lady Mary Wortley Montague was an accomplished writer of the 1700s. She traveled with her husband to Turkey. There she witnessed children being variolated. She was surprised that the smallpox they came down with was so mild. Lady Montague was especially interested in this method of preventing smallpox. She was a survivor of smallpox and had been badly scarred. Her brother had died from the disease. She decided to take the variolation technique back to England.

When she returned from Turkey, she tried to convince doctors that they should take up the practice. Smallpox had devastated England. The doctors ignored her pleas, perhaps because she was a woman. She didn't give up, though, and eventually convinced the royal family in England to become variolated. Soon everyone was doing it, and it saved countless lives.

Lady Mary Wortley Montague, a smallpox survivor, played a big part in the effort to protect people from the disease.

A Vaccine Is Born

In the late 1700s, a doctor named Edward Jenner noticed that women who milked cows or worked in dairies almost never got smallpox. These women, called milkmaids, did get a mild form of a related illness called cowpox, which they caught from the cows they milked. Jenner wondered whether getting cowpox made them immune to smallpox.

In 1796, Jenner decided to conduct an experiment. He took pus from the hand of a milkmaid with cowpox. He then injected it into an 8-year-old boy named James. Six weeks later, he exposed James to smallpox. James remained healthy, and thus the smallpox vaccine was born. The word vaccine comes from the Latin word *vacca*, which means "cow."

Jenner was overjoyed. He wrote in 1801 that this discovery had the potential to rid the world of smallpox forever. Yet the vaccination of large numbers of people was happening too slowly. The disease continued its path of destruction.

In 1967, the World Health Organization (WHO) planned to rid the world of smallpox once and for all through global vaccination. WHO would vaccinate every person on Earth who wasn't already vaccinated. Most of the United States and Europe were free of smallpox by this time, but the rest of the world was not. Whenever there was an outbreak of smallpox, medical teams rushed to the area on **behalf** of WHO to vaccinate people.

WHO was one of the few organizations that had the **capacity** to vaccinate large populations. During one outbreak of 12 people in New York City in 1947, 6 million people were vaccinated within a month. Over the following years, millions of people worldwide were vaccinated.

Ridding the World of a Disease

The last outbreak of smallpox in Europe occurred in 1972, in Yugoslavia. A man had traveled through Iraq, where there were still cases of smallpox. He contracted the disease without knowing it, and the disease quickly spread to friends and family. Officials of WHO were on the scene. They quarantined, or isolated, the victims to **prevent** any further spread. Anyone who had been exposed to someone who had smallpox was sent to a hotel, **accompanied** by armed guards, for 2 weeks. The people who were quarantined were left to watch each other for signs of the disease.

Doctors from around the world went to Yugoslavia to help. One recalls that he was shocked when he walked onto a hospital floor where the patients with active smallpox were kept. The patients had been abandoned by the local doctors, who had fled in terror. Nearly the whole population, about 18 million Yugoslavians, was eventually vaccinated.

A Somali man was one of the last people to get smallpox.

The last cured case of smallpox was in Somalia, in Africa, in 1977. The victim was a young man who had not been vaccinated. It is not generally known how he got the disease. Thousands of people nearby were immediately vaccinated. The disease had nowhere else to go. It had been defeated—or had it?

A year later, smallpox almost made a comeback in Europe because of an accident. In 1978, a medical photographer in Birmingham, England, was working in a university lab that contained the smallpox virus. Somehow the photographer became infected, but she didn't know it at the time. She had not been vaccinated. Later, she became ill. Her mother became infected as well. The photographer died, but her mother survived. To this day, no one can say exactly how the virus escaped from its sealed container in the lab to infect the photographer.

Finally, in 1980, WHO declared that it had rid the world of one of the most feared diseases of all time. At that time, there were several laboratories around the world that were keeping the live smallpox virus for an **indefinite** period of time for research. It was determined that only two samples of the virus would be kept, and the rest would be destroyed.

Some scientists feel that these virus samples should also be destroyed. They fear that somehow the live smallpox virus will escape. If that happened, there could be new cases of smallpox, possibly causing a **profusion** of cases. Other scientists argue that we need to have the virus for creating new vaccines, just in case smallpox makes a comeback.

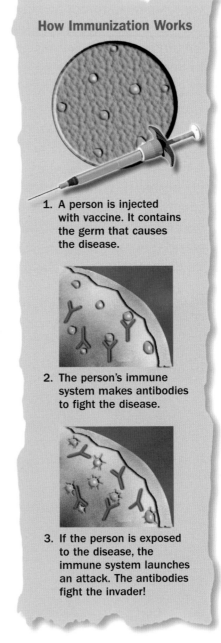

How Immunization Works

1. A person is injected with vaccine. It contains the germ that causes the disease.

2. The person's immune system makes antibodies to fight the disease.

3. If the person is exposed to the disease, the immune system launches an attack. The antibodies fight the invader!

When a disease is no longer a real threat, there's not much reason to vaccinate. The smallpox vaccine is no longer given. No one has been vaccinated for smallpox in the **preceding** 25 years. Another reason that smallpox vaccinations are not routinely given is that vaccinations are sometimes **accompanied** by bad side effects. The smallpox vaccine is more dangerous than other vaccines in this way. Efforts are being made to develop antiviral drugs that can be used to treat smallpox if the disease should ever reappear.

At this point, WHO receives information from governments about many diseases, including smallpox. If the disease should reappear, WHO can provide governments with information on how to diagnose smallpox and how to find sources of available vaccinations so people can be protected. Ridding the world of smallpox is an example of the success of medical science over the challenge of a deadly disease.

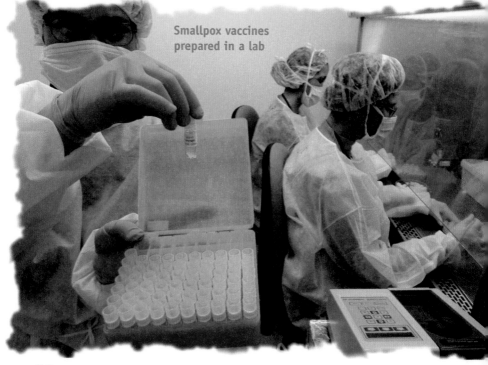

Smallpox vaccines
prepared in a lab

CHAPTER 4
Cholera

William Sproat was a boat worker in England. One evening, he felt slightly ill. He did not think too much of it. However, he had stomach cramps that doubled him over in pain throughout the night. The next day, he had cramps all over and lay in bed, barely moving. His pulse was weak. His eyes were sunken, his lips were blue, and he vomited **profusely**. In a few days, William Sproat died.

Sproat was England's first known victim of cholera. The year was 1831. Sproat's son also came down with the disease soon after his father and also died. Sproat's granddaughter caught it but survived. Soon, the whole town was infected, and within weeks the disease had spread throughout the countryside, leaving countless dead.

By the time cholera had reached England, it was already well known in many parts of the world. It first appeared in India in the 1500s. In the last two centuries, seven major cholera pandemics have swept the world.

Cholera is caused by a bacterial infection. It isn't spread through the air. People catch it by eating food or drinking water that has been contaminated by human waste. The main cause of death in cholera is dramatic fluid loss, which creates a dangerous imbalance in the body and shuts down the kidneys. The heart weakens and almost stops **circulating** blood through the body, and breathing may slow dramatically or increase rapidly. The infected person gets dehydrated, which means the body has lost too much fluid.

Some people miraculously survive this terrible illness. Some lucky people are naturally immune to cholera. The acid in their stomach is strong enough to kill the bacteria that cause cholera. Most people, though, are susceptible.

Children in Peru wait for clean drinking water.

Now that we know how people become infected with cholera, governments take precautions with the water supply and food safety. However, that was not always the case. In the 1800s, large amounts of human waste made their way into public water supplies. There was no plumbing at the time and no indoor toilets. In fact, in crowded cities, people used to dump their chamber pots, which held their waste, right out their windows. Passersby had to be sure to look up before walking by a building!

Cholera Epidemic

While the cholera epidemic raged in England in the 1830s, doctors watched helplessly. Many were convinced that miasma was causing the illness. However, a doctor named John Snow had a theory **contrary** to popular beliefs. He wondered how cholera could be caused by air and not affect the lungs. The disease struck the intestines, not the lungs. He began to suspect the water supply was to blame.

A district in London was suddenly hit hard by cholera. Snow found the well in that district that was most used by the residents. He convinced the townspeople to remove the handle from the pump. Sure enough, no one else in the district came down with cholera.

Despite the evidence, doctors still didn't believe Snow. In 1883, a German doctor, Robert Koch, actually identified the bacteria that cause cholera. Koch was one of the founders of the the germ theory of disease.

John Snow's discovery revolutionized the way major cities around the world handle sewage and water. We now know that sewage waste should not be mixed with drinking water. Snow made an enormous contribution to public health.

Cholera Today

However, there are still crowded villages and towns in underdeveloped countries where sewage is a problem, and it is difficult to find clean water. So, unfortunately, cholera is still a serious health problem. Some estimate that more than 75 percent of poor people who live in Africa, Asia, and South America don't have access to clean drinking water.

The danger of cholera also comes from tainted food. The bacteria that cause cholera can live for 2 to 5 days on meat and cheese and in milk. They can live up to 16 days on apples. Flies can carry the bacteria and contaminate food, blankets, and clothing.

A nineteenth-century cartoon shows the danger of London's public drinking water.

Cholera can also result after a natural disaster. If drinking water is polluted—by the inability to get clean water into the area or because of the presence of corpses and dirt—cholera is a major threat. For example, after the earthquake in Guatemala in 1976, three times as many people died of disease as from effects of the earthquake.

More recently, in the relief operations following the earthquake and tsunami of Southeast Asia and Africa, experts raced to prevent a possible outbreak of cholera. As relief workers tried to help survivors of the disaster, they knew that unsanitary conditions in the area could lead to an epidemic.

In the seven cholera pandemics, the disease had up to a 60 percent mortality rate. Today, the **outlook** for cholera victims is much better because doctors know how to treat the disease effectively. For example, a cholera patient must drink lots of fluids. The fluids must replace the fluids lost because of the disease. If patients are too weak to drink, they are given fluids through one of their veins. However, treatment must begin almost immediately because without treatment, death can come within 24 hours of the first symptoms.

In the United States, there have been a few cases of cholera in recent years brought in by Americans who traveled to South America. Once a person is infected, he or she can pass the illness along if hands are not properly washed after using the bathroom.

Modern sewage systems help to stop the spread of cholera, but these systems can't totally replace good hygiene. Modern science has given people information about how to avoid the dreaded disease and how to treat it successfully. It is up to people to use this information.

CHAPTER 5
The Flu of 1918

It was the middle of World War I. Young men from the United States went to Europe to fight enemy soldiers. There was another killer on the scene, though, besides the soldiers and their enemies. This killer was quieter than cannons but deadlier than any battle. In the end, it would kill more Americans than the battles of World War I, World War II, the Korean War, and the Vietnam War combined. It was the flu, or influenza. Yet it was like no flu ever seen before.

Masked volunteers feed children of families stricken with flu.

The most likely time to come down with the flu is in the winter. Most people get a fever and chest **congestion** for a week or two and then fully recover. Each year, however, a few people die from the flu, usually those who are elderly or very young. The flu of 1918 was different right from the beginning. For one thing, it took the lives of many healthy adults.

The flu of 1918 swept the globe in just a few months, the viruses **circulating** through the air from person to person. Initially seen in Spain, the flu of 1918 didn't seem so bad at first. A person suffered through 3 days of fever, aches, and pains. Then, the symptoms disappeared. Two months later, in a second wave, the flu **recurred**. This time it was deadly.

Those who came down with this second wave of flu, which is sometimes called the Spanish flu, suffered from a headache, burning eyes, and a raging fever that rose to more than 105°F. The victim would have trouble breathing, the face would turn purplish brown, and the feet would turn black. Soon, the victim would drown in the **congestion** of bloody fluid that filled the lungs. The process might take from one to several days.

This flu was contagious the way most influenzas are. A sneeze sprays droplets of virus through the air that are breathed in by another person. The flu can also be spread by getting the mucus of an infected person on your hands, say, by helping a child blow his or her nose and then touching your own nose or mouth.

The flu of 1918 was transmitted from one person to another more easily than most influenzas are. Worse, this flu was much more deadly. It killed more than 33,000 people in New York City alone. So many people died so quickly that hospital morgues were stacked with piles of bodies. Some Alaskan villages were almost completely wiped out, with only some of the children surviving, surrounded by the bodies of their parents.

Many countries reported huge numbers of flu deaths. The flu killed soldiers in trenches. It overwhelmed army camps. It struck cities hardest, where many people lived in a small area.

Some say it killed 21 million people worldwide within several months. Others say that that number is way too low an estimate because in India alone, 20 million people died. The number might be as high as 100 million people. It killed more people than any other single outbreak of a disease. Its death toll surpassed the Black Death. It was the deadliest human illness ever to hit the planet.

By the time of the flu of 1918, doctors knew about germs. So they guessed how the flu was spreading. Still, they didn't know what type of germ was causing it.

Many people in the medical world suspected that bacteria caused this sickness. Antibiotics hadn't been developed yet, but they wouldn't have helped anyway because the germs were viruses, not bacteria. Viruses are much smaller than bacteria. Microscopes powerful enough to see viruses had not yet been invented.

Efforts to save victims would have been **futile** in any case. Even today, most infections that are caused by a virus cannot be cured by taking medicine. Once you get such an infection, it just has to run its course. The course of this flu was short, but deadly.

During the pandemic, cities tried to put into place certain **external** measures that would help prevent the spread of the virus. People wore face masks in crowds at baseball games and other events or even just walking down the street. Yet there was little that could be done to stop the spread of the flu.

People did whatever they could to avoid the spread of the deadly flu—even on the baseball diamond!

63

The Pig Connection

After striking with shocking speed, the flu seemed to vanish as suddenly as it had appeared. However, during the 1918 flu pandemic, another species was being struck down by a flu. Pigs were dying in large numbers in the Midwest. No one thought to connect the two episodes until 10 years later.

Beginning in 1918, some pigs started coming down with flu each year. Called swine flu, the later versions weren't as deadly as the flu that had struck down people and pigs in 1918. Still, it was a problem for pig farmers. Scientists wondered if swine flu was the same flu that had taken such a toll on people as well as pigs in 1918.

When an influenza virus or any other virus attacks the body, antibodies form. Antibodies are how the body fights back and destroys the virus. Survivors of the 1918 flu were asked to donate blood to be tested for antibodies.

All the volunteers had flu antibodies in their blood. This blood was then tested against the swine flu virus that was still affecting pigs. Sure enough, these antibodies destroyed the swine flu virus. The effect of human antibodies on the swine flu virus meant that the swine flu and the Spanish flu were exactly or nearly exactly the same.

Did the flu of 1918 live on? If so, why weren't people getting sick from pigs and dying? Perhaps Spanish flu antibodies could destroy the swine flu virus, but swine flu antibodies wouldn't harm the Spanish flu virus.

Scientists realized they could only go so far without finding the killer virus itself. They needed to go back in time. They had to get hold of the flu virus of 1918.

Do pigs hold the answer to the spread of flu?

64

The Hunt for the Virus

During the flu of 1918, 500,000 Americans died. Two of the victims were young soldiers who had died in an army hospital. Doctors at the hospital had extracted some lung tissue from the soldiers soon after their death. The virus, preserved in wax, was sent to a warehouse in Washington, D.C. Nobody had thought to search for the sample, so it lay undisturbed for years.

In 1951, Dr. Johan Hultin, a Swedish medical student studying in the United States, had an idea. Many people in Alaska had died from the Spanish flu and had been buried in the permafrost, the permanently frozen earth. Hultin wondered if the virus also was preserved inside the lungs of those victims. If he could dig up the bodies, he might be able to get samples that still held the virus.

Hultin knew he could learn a lot if he were successful. Perhaps a vaccine could be made. However, there was a risk. What if he accidentally unleashed the pandemic all over again? Dr. Hultin decided to take a chance.

Dr. Hultin organized an expedition to northern Alaska and got permission from the villagers of Brevig to unearth the frozen bodies. He lit fires on the ground so the ice would melt, and he dug until he hit a body. Carefully, he removed tissue from several bodies and took samples back to his research facilities. **Contrary** to his hopes, not a single sample contained the virus. It was gone.

In 1976, a soldier in New Jersey died from the swine flu. Four other soldiers got sick with the swine flu but survived. Had the deadly flu of 1918 returned?

The fact that the swine flu had turned up in people frightened the medical community. Researchers decided that it was better to have a vaccine without an epidemic than an epidemic without a vaccine. So, **contrary** to the opinion of some doctors, the swine flu vaccine was given to 40 million Americans.

There was no epidemic. It had been a false alarm. No one other than those five soldiers ever came down with the swine flu, but lots of people claimed that the vaccine had made them ill. Some who got the vaccine died. No one could be sure if the vaccine had killed them. Americans had been vaccinated (at a cost of $135 million and several lost lives) for nothing. Meanwhile, the virus that caused the flu of 1918 was still unknown.

A breakthrough happened in 1997. Researchers wanted to study the genes of the 1918 virus to find out why it was such a deadly agent. Scientists were beginning to understand the genes of a wide variety of living things. They turned their attention to the Spanish flu virus. Remember the soldiers who had died from the flu? The slivers from their lungs were still sitting on a shelf in an army warehouse, preserved in wax. A researcher named Dr. Jeffery Taubenberger obtained them, and he and his staff were able to extract pieces of the now-dead virus from those old cubes of wax. However, they wanted to be sure that the samples of virus they had collected had not been altered by all those years in the wax.

Dr. Johan Hultin combed a mass grave to track down a virus.

That's when Dr. Hultin came back into the picture. He was now a retired doctor in his 70s. He went back to Alaska to see if he could retrieve more samples in the hopes of finding some that still contained the virus.

Again, Hultin gained permission from the Brevig villagers, opened up the earth, and dug into the permafrost. Again, he came upon bodies. Most of them were **visibly** decomposed at this point. The corpse of one woman, lying next to a collection of bones, was still intact. Because the woman had been such a heavy person when she was alive, a thick layer of fat had helped to preserve the woman's flesh and internal organs.

Hultin removed the woman's lungs and placed frozen slices of them in containers to ship off to Taubenberger. The lung tissue was shown to have traces of the virus. Genetic tests confirmed what the **preceding** analysis of tissue samples had shown—the 1918 flu virus.

Bird Flu?

The genes of the terrible flu of 1918 confirm something strange. The deadly virus was originally a bird flu. Usually, people are immune to bird flu. Somehow the virus had changed so that it could live in humans. It might have jumped from birds to pigs to people.

Pigs can carry both bird and human strains of influenza. If pigs become infected with both at the same time, the viruses could mutate into a new influenza that is able to survive in people.

There have been two other flu pandemics since 1918: the Asian flu of 1957 and the Hong Kong flu of 1968–1969. Together these two pandemics resulted in the deaths of 4 million to 5 million people worldwide. The viruses of the Asian flu and the Hong Kong flu may also have originated in birds.

Recently, there have been cases of humans coming down with a bird flu that they caught from infected chickens. Preparing infected chickens for cooking is one way people can get the flu.

Bird flu (also called avian flu) is becoming more and more common among poultry. Cases of bird flu have even been found in poultry in North America. To prevent the spread of bird flu from chickens to people, all infected chickens must be destroyed. All flocks that have a few infected chickens among them are destroyed as well. There is also a vaccine that chicken farmers can give to their flocks to protect them. The first stage of containing the bird flu is to keep poultry from getting it.

Researchers use their knowledge about bird flu to learn more on **behalf** of the human population. Researchers are in the process of developing a vaccine to protect people from getting the bird flu. The goal is first to make a vaccine that works and then to produce it in enough quantity to vaccinate Earth's entire human population. It may not be long before the bird flu vaccine is available and at the ready in case there is danger of a pandemic.

Connections among animals and humans lead to the spread of influenza.

CHAPTER 6
Modern Epidemics

Imagine if a new virus suddenly arose that attacked human beings and was as deadly or even deadlier than the viruses you have read about. Think about what it would take to contain the virus in time. Would we be able to develop a vaccine fast enough to save people?

In 1976, a new family of viruses began emerging from the African rain forests. These viruses are called filoviruses, or thread-shaped viruses. The different filoviruses all look alike, as if they are closely related. They also look like no other known viruses on Earth. These viruses create in the human body a similar bloody fever, an illness that destroys the body from the inside out. When a filovirus attacks, it invades a body's red blood cells and begins to make copies of itself. Soon, the body is full of viruses.

The story of the Ebola virus began in a small town in Sudan, Africa, along the Ebola River, in 1976. There, a cotton factory employee became ill. His eyes grew **visibly** red, he had a raging fever, and his lungs began to fill with blood. He began to vomit blood. Then he began to bleed **grotesquely** through every opening in his body. When someone dies from a filovirus, it is said that that person "crashed and bled." No one knew what had happened to the man or how he got sick, but soon two of his co-workers developed the same symptoms.

Many people in the town got sick, too. They were taken to a local hospital where they were given shots to help them feel better. The hospital didn't have enough needles, so staff members reused the needles the hospital had. Soon the disease, whatever it was, had jumped from hospital bed to hospital bed, room to room.

Before long, the whole hospital had become a morgue. The victims all developed red eyes, vomited blood, and eventually bled **profusely** through every opening in their bodies. They went into shock, and many died. Then, as mysteriously as it came, the sickness, called Ebola Sudan, left. Half of the people who were hospitalized with Ebola Sudan had died—in other words, the virus had a 50 percent mortality rate.

A filovirus jumps from body to body mainly through blood. For example, if a doctor gets splashed with blood from a patient infected with the Ebola virus and it enters his or her mouth, eyes, or a small cut on the hand, he or she will come down with the sickness. Filoviruses are dangerous and powerful. If you are infected, you will come down with the disease.

In 1980, another of the filovirus varieties emerged, also causing a bloody fever. This time it was in a man who had spent time in a particular cave called Kitum in Kenya, Africa. This virus was called Marburg, named for the German city where the virus first appeared. It was the second known filovirus. Marburg has a 25 percent mortality rate, making it the least deadly of the filoviruses.

Seven years later, a young boy explored the same cave. Many people had explored the cave since 1980, but no one else had gotten sick. However, this boy came down with the virus and died. Is it possible that the Marburg virus lives in the cave? Maybe the bats that live in the cave are carriers, or an unknown insect spreads the disease in its bite. To this day, no one knows. However, it is suspected that something in that cave has the **capacity** to cause the deadly illness.

Did cave-dwelling bats
spread Marburg virus?

Yet Another Filovirus

Two months after the Sudan
outbreak in 1976, another virus
emerged, this time in the African
country that was then called Zaire.

No one knows who was the first person to
have this virus. However, the sickness, called Ebola
Zaire, that was caused by the virus first surfaced in a
hospital clinic run by nuns. The nuns gave the people of
the village injections, including vaccines and antibiotics,
with needles that hadn't been sterilized. They went from
person to person, giving shots without cleaning the
needles in between.

Ebola Zaire is very infectious. Only a small amount of virus in a drop of blood is needed to infect a person. Soon, people in the surrounding villages were dying, especially the people who had received the shots and members of their families. They all died of massive bleeding, internal and external. The virus that causes Ebola Zaire is the deadliest of all the filoviruses. It has a mortality rate of 90 percent—for every 10 people with the filovirus, 9 die.

When the filovirus attacks, it invades a body's **circulatory** system and begins to make copies of itself. Ebola Zaire attacks every organ and tissue in the body. Often victims die in a spasm, or fit, thrashing around, spraying everyone around them with blood. That blood contains the killer virus and is deadly to touch.

There have been **recurring** outbreaks of Ebola in Africa. Specialists who work on **behalf** of affected populations are sent to investigate outbreaks of infectious diseases in these places. Each time, the outbreaks aren't widespread. However, there is recent evidence that Ebola Zaire can spread through droplets in the air.

Gravediggers in Zaire

AIDS

What will be the epidemic of the twenty-first century? It may be a disease that is already here. AIDS, which stands for acquired immunodeficiency syndrome, may well be this century's most serious epidemic. It is one of the deadliest diseases in human history.

There are 42 million people infected worldwide with the AIDS virus today. Each year, more than 3 million people die of AIDS. The first cases of AIDS in the United States were identified more than 20 years ago. Now, there are estimated to be almost a million Americans who may be infected.

What exactly is AIDS, and how did it become such a huge problem? AIDS is caused by the human immunodeficiency virus (HIV). As the virus **circulates** through the bloodstream, it attacks a body's immune system. It damages the body's **capacity** to fight off infections.

The first symptoms of HIV appear a month or two after the virus enters the body. Those signs include fever, headache, fatigue, and swollen glands. Then the signs disappear. A person with HIV may feel fine for 10 years or more and not even know he or she has it. However, during this time the virus is multiplying, and the person is contagious. If the virus leads to AIDS, the next stages can be weight loss, a return of fatigue, rashes, memory loss, infections, and even a cancer that the body can't fight. Often people who have AIDS die of pneumonia because they are unable to fight off the pneumonia infection.

However, not every person with HIV develops AIDS. Some people have lived with HIV for many years. Drugs have been helpful in slowing down the disease. Currently, there isn't a cure for HIV or for AIDS.

AIDS doesn't kill overnight like the flu of 1918. It can take many years for a person to die of AIDS—enough time, victims hope, for researchers to find a cure.

FACTS ABOUT AIDS

AIDS is caused by HIV.

Millions of Americans have HIV, and some of them have AIDS.

Today, there are no cures or vaccines that can prevent AIDS.

New treatments enable people with AIDS to live longer.

AIDS can be **prevented** by avoiding risky behaviors.

We still don't know for sure how AIDS started, but we do know how it spreads. People can get AIDS from sexual contact, and as with the Ebola virus, from the exchange of blood. In many countries today, doctors and nurses are very careful to use only clean needles to give shots or draw blood. However, in many poor countries that isn't always the case, and drug users sometimes spread AIDS by sharing dirty needles. AIDS workers travel all over the world to educate people about **preventing** AIDS.

AIDS used to be transmitted through blood transfusions. Sometimes when people undergo surgery, they need to be given extra blood. Before health organizations knew about AIDS, blood supplies were not always safe. Sometimes people were unknowingly given blood that was infected with the virus. Now blood supplies are very safe, so the disease is not transmitted that way.

So far, some drugs have been developed that slow the virus down, and these drugs improve the **outlook** for patients with AIDS. Some new drugs greatly reduce the number of viruses in the bloodstream. People can remain healthier for longer, even though there is no cure, and no vaccine exists. The only sure way to survive AIDS is through **prevention**.

Beware of Mosquitoes

For as long as people have lived in tropical places, mosquitoes have infected them with diseases such as malaria, which causes **recurrent** fevers. The germs' hosts are people and mosquitoes. These hosts work on **behalf** of the disease without realizing it.

When a mosquito carrying malaria bites a person, the germs of the disease enter the person's **circulatory** system. There they live in the red blood cells. The germs may create a fever in the host to break up any clumps of red blood cells so the germs can drift freely in the bloodstream. When the next mosquito bites the infected person, the germs are in place in the blood and are sucked up by the mosquito. There, inside the insect, they multiply. When the mosquito bites the next victim, malaria germs are ready to infect someone new.

Some mosquito-borne illnesses have recently arrived in the United States. One of these illnesses is the West Nile fever. The virus that causes this illness has been a problem in Africa since the late 1930s. A few years ago, the West Nile virus was found in birds, horses, and people in the United States.

Symptoms for the West Nile fever vary. Most people will have no symptoms at all. Some will vomit and have a fever, a headache, and sometimes a rash. They might be sick for a few days or weeks. A few people will get very sick, though. They may have vision loss, shake uncontrollably, and even go into a coma.

Health-care officials tell people to avoid being bitten by mosquitoes. In warm weather, people should remove standing water, use insect repellent, and keep screens on open windows and doors. By taking these precautions, people can avoid getting the West Nile fever.

SARS

Another dangerous disease, which is not spread by insects like the ones in the **preceding** discussion, has arrived on the scene in recent years. This disease is called severe acute respiratory syndrome (SARS). First reported in China, cases of SARS started appearing around the world, including in Canada and the United States. Symptoms begin with a high fever, body aches, and **congested** lungs or a dry cough. Then pneumonia develops.

After the first outbreak of SARS, WHO issued a global health alert, advising anyone showing symptoms not to travel. As mentioned above, SARS isn't carried by insects. It can only be transmitted by breathing in infected droplets from a sneeze or cough. SARS is caused by a virus that the medical field has never seen before in people or animals. SARS was first reported in China. However, the ultimate source of the virus is still unknown.

WHO immediately sent medical teams to hospitals in China and in other countries in Southeast Asia to work with doctors to stop the disease. A full-blown epidemic didn't occur, but if it does in the future, we should be ready. Experts have improved infection-control procedures that should **prevent** spread of the disease.

Knowledge has increased since the days of the Black Death, when people had no idea how and why disease spreads. We know much more today about causes, treatments, and **prevention**. Germs, though tiny, can pose a threat to human life. However, armed with information, vaccinations, and treatments, scientists have made enormous progress in controlling or eliminating many diseases. For those diseases that cannot yet be cured, research continues. Scientists are studying the germs and applying knowledge gained from past successes in order to meet the challenge of conquering other diseases.

Glossary

accompanied went along with or joined in an action. **Accompanying** means going along with or belonging to.

apparently seemingly

behalf in the interest or aid of. "On **behalf** of" means as a representative for.

capacity the ability to perform; also, the maximum amount that can be contained or accommodated

circulates passes from place to place or moves in a path. The **circulatory** system moves blood through the body.

circumstances facts or events connected in some way with a situation

congestion excessive fullness or stuffiness

contrary the opposite; as opposed to

disadvantage anything that stands in the way of success

economic having to do with money, business, or industry. **Economy** means the managing of money spent in a home, business, region, or country.

elusive difficult to catch or see; able to avoid capture. **Elude** means to avoid capture or to escape or get away from.

evolving slowly developing or changing. **Evolve** means to slowly develop or change.

exotic from another part of the world; unusual or different

externally on the outside of. **External** means outward.

formidable causing fear or alarm; difficult to defeat

futile useless, unsuccessful; not able to produce a result

grotesque odd or unnatural in appearance; weird

impose to put on someone as a duty, burden, or penalty; to force oneself on others or on a place. **Imposing** means putting a burden on someone.

indefinitely without a fixed or an exact limit; going on and on. **Indefinite** means an inexact amount of time or number.

interact to act on each other. **Interacting** means acting on each other. **Interactions** means actions on each other.

outlook the view from a particular place; prospect(s) for the future

perspective a way of looking at something

preceding going before, coming ahead of; the thing that comes before or goes first

predators animals that survive by eating other animals. **Predatory** means living by capturing or feeding upon other animals.

predicament an unpleasant or difficult situation that is hard to find a way out of

prevention the act of keeping something from happening. **Preventive** means used to stop something from happening.

profusion a great quantity of something. **Profusely** means in large amounts.

recur to happen again, to return. **Recurrence** means the act of happening again.

robust full of health and strength; vigorous

sustain to keep alive; to support; to keep from falling or sinking

visibly clearly, easily seen

vitality good health; energy. **Vital** means very important.